THOMAS EDISON

By Richard Hantula

WORLD ALMANAC® LIBRARY

Please visit our web site at: www.worldalmanaclibrary.com
For a free color catalog describing World Almanac® Library's list
of high-quality books and multimedia programs, call 1-800-848-2928 (USA)
or 1-800-387-3178 (Canada). World Almanac® Library's fax: (414) 332-3567.

Library of Congress Cataloging-in-Publication Data

Hantula, Richard.
    Thomas Edison / by Richard Hantula.
        p. cm. — (Trailblazers of the modern world)
    Includes bibliographical references and index.
    ISBN 0-8368-5496-9 (lib. bdg.)
    ISBN 0-8368-5265-6 (softcover)
    1. Edison, Thomas A. (Thomas Alva), 1847-1931—Juvenile literature. 2. Electric engineers—
United States—Biography—Juvenile literature. 3. Inventors—United States—Biography—Juvenile
literature. I. Title. II. Series.
TK140.E3H36   2004
621.3'092—dc22
[B]   2004041269

First published in 2005 by
World Almanac® Library
330 West Olive Street, Suite 100
Milwaukee, WI 53212 USA

Project manager: Jonny Brown
Editor: Alan Wachtel
Design and page production: Scott M. Krall
Photo research: Diane Laska-Swanke
Indexer: Walter Kronenberg

Photo credits: © Bettmann/CORBIS: 4 bottom, 7, 9, 12, 20, 24, 30, 31, 43; © Bohemian Nomad Picturemakers/
CORBIS: 34; © CORBIS: 11, 13, 14, 23, 29, 35; © Hulton Archive/Getty Images: cover, 4 top, 8, 10, 15, 16, 17,
19, 21, 22, 28, 33, 38, 42; © Schenectady Museum; Hall of Electrical History Foundation/CORBIS: 5, 25, 39, 40;
© David E. Scherman/Time Life Pictures/Getty Images: 18; © Joseph Sohm; ChromoSohm Inc./CORBIS: 27;
© John Springer Collection/CORBIS: 32; © Underwood & Underwood/CORBIS: 37

Printed in the United States of America

1 2 3 4 5 6 7 8 9 08 07 06 05 04

TABLE of CONTENTS

Words that appear in the glossary are printed in **boldface**
type the first time they occur in the text.

CHAPTER 1

THE WIZARD OF INVENTION

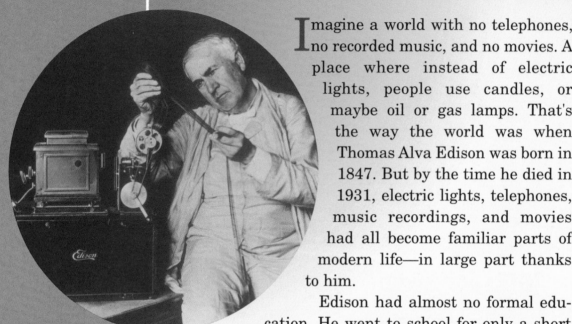

Thomas Edison examining film from one of his movie projectors

Edison invented the first practical lightbulb.

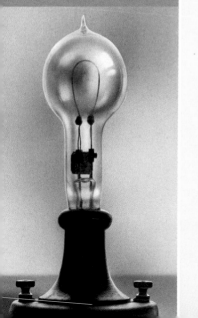

Imagine a world with no telephones, no recorded music, and no movies. A place where instead of electric lights, people use candles, or maybe oil or gas lamps. That's the way the world was when Thomas Alva Edison was born in 1847. But by the time he died in 1931, electric lights, telephones, music recordings, and movies had all become familiar parts of modern life—in large part thanks to him.

Edison had almost no formal education. He went to school for only a short period, perhaps as brief as a few months, when he was a boy, and for most of his life he was extremely hard of hearing. But he had great curiosity, an ability to see connections between things that others might miss, and a love of working hard. Edison was able to teach himself what he needed to know, and he developed into an enormously creative inventor. Along the way, he also became a prominent businessman who played a role in the formation of many companies that eventually became part of General Electric, one of the most powerful corporations in the world. In 1997, *Life* magazine put Edison at the top of its list of the most important people of the previous millennium—that is, of the past one thousand years. Edison, said *Life*, "gave humans the power to create light without fire, by inventing a long-lasting, affordable **incandescent lamp**."

Business Leader

A great number of companies were established by Edison, his associates, and others to develop, manufacture, and sell his inventions. Many of these companies bore his name, as did many other firms that had no connection with his inventions but used his name, sometimes illegally, because of people's willingness to buy almost anything called "Edison." Here are a few of the U.S. electrical-industry companies in which Edison played some role:

•Bergmann & Company: created in 1881, it made electric lighting fixtures, sockets, and other devices used with Edison's electric lighting system.

•Edison Electric Illuminating Company of New York: established in 1880 to build generating stations in New York City, its first product was the historic Pearl Street station.

•Edison Electric Light Company: organized in 1878, this company helped fund Edison's electric light experiments.

•Edison Lamp Works: beginning production of lamps in 1880, this company changed its name in 1881, first to Edison Electric Lamp Company and then to Edison Lamp Company.

•Edison Machine Works: established in 1881, this company made **dynamos** and big electric motors for the Edison electric light system.

In 1889, the Edison General Electric Company was established through a merger of Bergmann & Company, Edison Electric Light Company, Edison Lamp Company, and Edison Machine Works. The Edison General Electric Company merged with the Thomson-Houston Electric Company, another maker of electrical equipment, in 1892, to form the General Electric Company.

The Edison Machine Works at Schenectady, N.Y., around 1886

Of course, some people might object to naming a person who worked in science or **technology** as the most significant individual of the last millennium. What about great political leaders, or military leaders, or explorers, or writers? Some critics even might object to picking Edison instead of any of a number of other persons in the area of science and technology who produced major inventions and, unlike Edison, also made several important scientific discoveries. And, in objection to crediting Edison with the invention of the electric lightbulb, some critics might bring up that Edison was not the only person to contribute to its development.

But Edison is generally credited with making the first practical incandescent light, and much more besides. He received a total of 1,093 U.S. patents for his inventions—more than any other person in history. It is no accident that the invention most often associated with his name—the lightbulb—is often used by cartoonists as a symbol for a good idea or a flash of inspiration. Among the many other items that Edison either invented or improved are the **telegraph**, telephone, phonograph, movie camera, and **storage battery**. He is the father of the sound-recording and motion picture industries.

R & D

Perhaps the most important thing Edison invented was not a device at all but a method for inventing. He began as, and always remained, a "hands on" inventor who loved to spend endless hours working on whatever problem interested him. But he believed that the best way to make progress was to have a well-equipped laboratory staffed by a team of people with different skills and talents who could help him conduct a systematic study of a

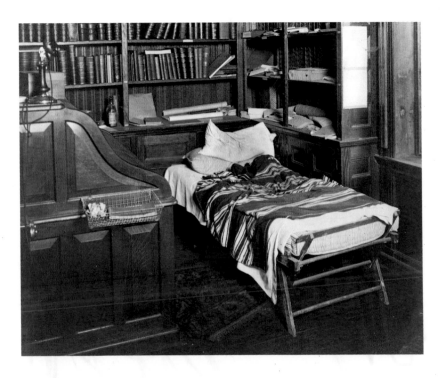

problem. He introduced the industrial research and development, or "R&D," laboratory, in which more than one problem could be studied at a time. Edison's major labs were forerunners of the massive R&D laboratories that are today an essential part of important corporations such as General Electric and General Motors. It was because he had an R&D team at his disposal that, in 1882, the number of **patent** applications that he filed (and were later approved) reached the amazing total of 106—the greatest number of patents he applied for in a single year. "One of Edison's greatest overlooked talents," historian Greg Field says, "was his ability to assemble teams and set up an organizational structure that fostered many people's creativity."

When a problem attracted Edison's interest, his natural curiosity and thoroughness pushed him to explore it from many sides, often leading to the creation of many devices and improvements instead of just one. For example, 150 of his patents concern the telegraph,

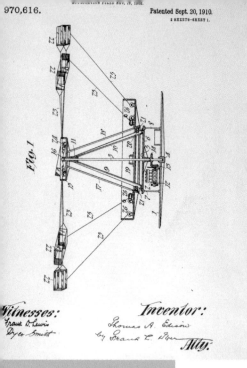

Fig.1

Witnesses:
Frank D. Lewis
Dyer Smith

Inventor:
Thomas A. Edison
by Frank L. Dyer
Atty.

A drawing from a patent application Edison filed in 1908 for "certain new and useful Improvements in Flying-Machines"

and well over 350 fall into the category of electric light and power. When he developed a practical lightbulb, electric-power distribution systems did not yet exist. Edison understood that people could not use his lightbulbs without easily available electric power, so he worked up an entire system for distributing and using electric power. Emil Rathenau, an electrical engineer who founded the German General Electric Company, described the impressive results: "The Edison system of lighting was as beautifully conceived down to the very last details, and as thoroughly worked out as if it had been tested for decades in various towns. Neither sockets, switches, fuses, lampholders, or any of other accessories were wanting; and the generation of the current, the regulation, the wiring

Edison's Patents

A patent on an invention represents the legal right to make or sell that invention. This right belongs only to the holder of the patent. According to a breakdown published by the Henry Ford Museum & Greenfield Village in Dearborn, Michigan, the 1,093 patents issued to Edison, or to Edison together with others, fall into these general categories:

Category	Number of patents	Category	Number of patents
Telegraph	150	Automobile	8
Electric pen and mimeograph	5	Typewriter	3
Telephone	34	Vacuum preservation	1
Phonograph	195	Autogiro (a type of aircraft	
Electric light and power	389	similar to a helicopter)	1
Railroad	25	Chemicals	3
Ore separator	62	Military projectiles	3
Cement	40	Radio	2
Motion pictures	9	Rubber	1
Battery	141	Miscellaneous	21

with distributing-boxes, house-connections, meters, etc., all showed signs of astonishing skill."

Another aspect of Edison's amazing productivity was that he commonly tackled several different projects at the same time. Even during the busiest period of his work on the complicated electric-lighting problem, he also devised a new type of telephone receiver and developed a technique for separating metal ore from rock. His experiences in one area sometimes proved useful in dealing with a different one. Ideas and techniques that were tried in one project might be reused in others, sometimes years later. Edison kept track of his projects and his never-ending flow of ideas by constantly taking notes. Many of these are contained in the about 3,500 notebooks of Edison's that historians have preserved.

Edison poses for the movie camera outside his lab in West Orange, N.J.

INVENTION FACTORY

Edison built his first big research and development laboratory in 1876 in a little village called Menlo Park, located in New Jersey about 25 miles (40 kilometers) southwest of New York City. At the time, it was the biggest private technological laboratory in the United States. He called it an "invention factory," in which he expected to make "a minor invention every ten days and a big thing every six months or so." As a result of the publicity he received for the products of the lab, newspapers began calling Edison "the Wizard of Menlo Park."

In 1887, Edison built a much bigger facility in West Orange, N.J., about 15 miles (25 kilometers) west of New York City. He planned for it to "have the best equipped and largest Laboratory extant. . . . In fact there is no similar institution in existence." At the West Orange lab, as many as two hundred people worked in facilities designed for the "rapid and cheap development of an invention, and working it up into commercial shape." Around the lab there gradually arose factories for mass production of some of Edison's commercially successful inventions. The number of people working in the factories grew as high as 10,000 in 1919–1920.

Edison with one of his inventions at his West Orange lab

CHAPTER 2

THE BOY WHO LIKED TO ASK QUESTIONS

The Edison family has old roots in New Jersey. In the eighteenth century, Thomas Edison's great-grandfather John Edeson (as the name, which was Dutch, was once spelled) owned land in New Jersey, close to where Edison's grand West Orange lab would stand more than a century later. Edeson, however, supported the British during the American Revolution, and the family was forced to move to Canada in 1784. They eventually made a home in Ontario.

Edison's father, Samuel Ogden Edison Jr., and his mother, Nancy Mathews Elliott, a schoolteacher born in the state of New York, married in Ontario and started a family. Samuel took part in an uprising against the government in 1837; when the revolt was crushed, he fled to the United States. He settled in 1839 in the town of Milan, in northern Ohio, where he was joined by his wife and the couple's four children. Three more children were born in Milan; the last of them was Thomas Alva, on February 11, 1847. Of the seven brothers and sisters, three died in childhood.

Milan in those days was linked by canal with a river that flowed into Lake Erie, and the town was a prosperous grain-shipping port. The Edisons lived in a three-story house that was built by Samuel, who worked as a shingle maker.

Edison as a young boy

Little Thomas Alva was usually called "Al." (Later, by the time he was fourteen or so, he preferred "Tom.") He was a mischievous boy, now and then getting into trouble. It is said that Al once fell into the canal and had to be pulled out. In another escapade, he vanished inside a grain elevator (a storage building for grain), and was nearly smothered before he was saved. In 1853, one story goes, he started a fire in his father's barn "just to see what it would do." The barn burned down, earning Al a whipping from his father in the village square. Al's father did not know what to make of his son, who seemed to lack common sense but was curious about things and was constantly asking "foolish questions."

Edison in the chemistry section of his West Orange lab

MICHIGAN, AND A LITTLE SCHOOLING

When a railroad was built in northern Ohio, Milan's canal traffic decreased, and it became harder to make a living in the town. In 1854, the Edison family moved to Port Huron, Michigan, where Samuel worked in various lines of business. Al went to a private school for a brief period and later for a short while attended the Port Huron Union School. Several reasons have been suggested for why he had so little formal schooling. School was expensive for a family like his, which had little money—a small fee had to be paid even for the public Union School. It is also known that Al was often sick as a child, and he may have already started to suffer from partial deafness. While in school, he apparently was a poor student and did not pay attention in class. According to one story, a teacher described him as "addled" (confused) and not worth keeping in school. This, the story goes, upset Al and angered his mother so much that she began educating him at home.

Tom Edison at age fourteen

It seems definite that Edison got most of his education at home from his mother, a former schoolteacher. He later recalled, "My mother was the making of me. She was so true, so sure of me, and I felt I had some one to live for, some one I must not disappoint." He also read a lot, including books on history and other subjects that his mother gave him or that were in his father's library. One favorite of his was a science textbook used at the Union School: *A School Compendium of Natural and Experimental Philosophy*, by Richard Parker. The book covered subjects such as physics and astronomy. It also contained sections on topics such as the steam engine and the telegraph, and it included a chart of the **Morse code**. When Al was about twelve—perhaps about the time he read Parker's book—he built a telegraph line half a mile (about a kilometer) long from his house to a friend's house. Besides electrical devices such as the telegraph, he was also interested in chemistry, and started collecting chemicals, which his mother made him keep in the basement after she decided he was turning his room into a mess. Many years later, his father, Samuel, said about Al, "He spent the greater part of his time in the cellar. He did not share to any extent the sports of his neighborhood. He never knew a real boyhood like other boys."

WORKING ON THE RAILROAD

An artist's impression of young Tom Edison saving the stationmaster's little son

Edison helped out on his father's garden, but he didn't particularly like that kind of work, because he found it tedious and he didn't like working in the sun. In 1859, a Grand Trunk Railway line between Port Huron and Detroit opened, and Edison persuaded his mother to let him get a job selling newspapers and candy on the train. He was allowed to put a printing press in the baggage car, and in the spring of 1862, he used it to publish a newspaper called the Weekly Herald. He also had a small chemical laboratory in the baggage car, where he carried out experiments. After a fire accidentally broke out, however, his lab was removed from the train.

In another incident in 1862, Edison moved the three-year-old son of stationmaster James MacKenzie out of the path of an oncoming freight car. MacKenzie rewarded Edison by teaching him how to operate a telegraph. Even with his poor hearing, Edison could hear the high-pitched sound produced by the telegraph.

Hard of Hearing

Edison's hearing apparently became much worse during the period when he was working on the train. He later wrote in his diary, "I haven't heard a bird sing since I was 12 years old." What caused his increasing deafness is unknown. It could have been an inherited condition, or perhaps it was an aftereffect of illness—Edison had scarlet fever as a child. Edison himself thought his deafness was triggered when a conductor lifted him onto a train by picking him up by the ears.

Edison claimed that his partial deafness was beneficial to him. Because he couldn't hear many sounds or noises that might have bothered people with normal hearing, it was easier for him to think and to concentrate on his work. His poor hearing, however, was a hindrance to his work on inventions involving sound. In order to hear a phonograph or piano, he often bit into it; his teeth picked up the sound vibrations, which traveled to his inner ear, a part of his hearing system that still functioned. In spite of his hearing problem, Edison himself often selected the performers for his music phonograph records.

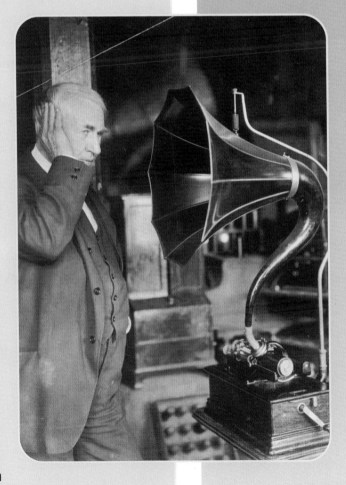

Edison, with his poor hearing, attempts to listen to a phonograph.

CHAPTER 3

EARLY INNOVATIONS

On his 81st birthday, the famous former telegraph operator pushes a telegraph key to officially launch a new lighting system.

In early 1863, Edison—by then usually called "Tom"—got his first job as a telegraph operator at the little telegraph office in Port Huron. Looking for more challenging work, he applied to the Grand Trunk Railway and was given a job as a nighttime operator at Stratford Junction, Ontario, which was about 75 miles (120 kilometers) north of Port Huron. This was his first real job away from home. For the next few years he worked as a "tramp telegrapher," moving from job to job in different cities. Among the places where he worked by 1867 were Adrian, Michigan; Fort Wayne, Indiana; Indianapolis, Indiana; Cincinnati, Ohio; Memphis, Tennessee; and Louisville, Kentucky.

In those years, Edison became a highly skilled telegraph operator, able to quickly and in very clear handwriting write down the messages he received. But on more than one occasion he was fired. He spent much of his time reading technical and scientific books and magazines and doing experiments to learn more about how the telegraph worked and to find ways of improving it. He sometimes used equipment belonging to the companies he worked for, but he also purchased materials with his own money. A friend of his in Memphis later remembered, "He spent his money buying apparatus and books, and wouldn't buy clothing. That winter he went without an overcoat and nearly froze."

A USEFUL LESSON

In 1868, the twenty-one-year-old Edison got a job as an operator in Boston, Massachusetts, at the main office of the Western Union Telegraph Company, which was one of the leading telegraph companies in the United States. It was a good opportunity for a young man who wanted to develop new electrical devices. Boston was a big city where he could meet other inventors, skilled mechanics who could help him build equipment, and businessmen with enough money to help finance his inventions.

Edison was particularly interested in telegraph devices, but he also had ideas for other inventions. In October 1868, he completed the application for a patent

Faraday

Edison was greatly influenced by the British scientist Michael Faraday (1791-1867), who made important discoveries about electricity and magnetism. One of the books Edison studied during his years as a telegraph operator was Faraday's *Experimental Researches in Electricity.* Edison regarded Faraday as a "Master Experimenter." Like Edison, Faraday was self-taught. Another similarity between Faraday and Edison was that both tended to avoid using mathematics in their work.

on an electric vote-counting machine for use in legislative bodies, such as Congress or state legislatures. The patent, which was issued in June of the following year, was the first he ever received. To his disappointment, no one wanted to buy the device. Lawmakers, Edison discovered, were not interested in speeding up the counting of their votes. For them, the slow process of recording legislators' votes one-by-one in a roll call had certain advantages. The automatic vote recorder was shown to a committee of Congress, whose chairman reportedly told Edison, "Young man, that is just what we do not want. Your invention would destroy the only hope that the minority would have of influencing legislation. . . . And as the ruling majority knows that at some day they may become a minority, they will be as much averse to change as their opponents." Edison later recalled that he "was as much crushed as it was possible to be at my age." But the incident was a useful lesson for him. It helped persuade him that if he hoped to make a career as an inventor, he would need to focus on things that were likely to be in "commercial demand."

One of Edison's early inventions was a stock ticker—that is, a printing telegraph for stock quotations.

STARTING A BUSINESS

In early 1869, Edison quit his job as an operator at Western Union in order to "devote his full time to bringing out his inventions," and a few months later he moved to New York City. New York and neighboring New Jersey were to be his main base of operations for the rest of his life. He opened his first sizable shop for making equipment in 1870. It was located in Newark, New Jersey, not far from New York City. Most of his projects during his Newark years concerned improvements in telegraph technology. Among them were telegraph printers, automatic telegraph equipment, a "double transmitter" that could send two messages at a time on the same wire, and a "quadruplex" capable of sending two messages at a time in opposite directions. By the middle of the 1870s, Edison had the reputation as the top telegraph inventor in the United States. Some called him a genius.

Edison in the 1870s

But as usual, Edison's interests extended far and wide. Another of his notable early inventions was the so-called electric pen, which he initially developed in 1875. The electric pen provided a way of easily making many copies of an original document. When you "wrote" on a piece of paper with the pen, it made tiny holes in the paper, which could then be used as a stencil for making additional copies.

A Demanding Boss

Edison worked tremendously hard. He expected those who worked for him to put in overtime if the need arose. In one case during the early 1870s, the need for overtime arose when Edison got a rush order for some of the telegraph printers he manufactured in those years. Unfortunately, the printers that were ordered were a model he had just developed, and the design had bugs. Edison told six of his men that he and they would remain at the lab until they figured out the problems. "Now, you fellows," he said, "I've locked the door, and you'll have to stay here until this job is completed. Well, let's find the bugs." They did it, but it took sixty hours of work with no sleep and not much food.

Although Edison was absorbed in his inventing and related business problems, family matters became important in 1871. Edison's mother died in April. Three years had passed since he had last seen her, and he traveled to Port Huron for the funeral. Later that year, Edison proposed marriage to one of his employees, Mary Stilwell, a sixteen-year-old clerk from Newark. She accepted, and the two quickly got married, on Christmas Day of that year. They made their home in Newark. A daughter, Marion Estelle, was born in February 1873, and a son, Thomas Jr., in January 1876. Edison nicknamed Marion "Dot" and Thomas Jr. "Dash," after the two types of signals used in telegraphers' Morse code.

Edison loved his wife. But he also loved his work. He was not used to family life, and his inventing so absorbed him that he would spend up to eighteen hours a day at work and sometimes even slept there rather than coming home. According to legend, Edison went back to his workshop right after he and Mary were married. He seems to have been surprised and disappointed when he discovered that Mary was not capable of helping him in his work. A little over a month after the wedding, he wrote in one of his notebooks, "Mrs Mary Edison My wife Dearly Beloved Cannot invent worth a Damn!!" On Valentine's Day, he wrote, "My Wife Popsy Wopsy Can't Invent."

Two of Edison's children have a reading lesson at home.

CHAPTER 4

SOUND AND LIGHT

Edison's "invention factory" in Menlo Park, New Jersey, was built in early 1876 under the supervision of his father. The Edison family themselves moved to the village in March. The lab became the site of two of Edison's most historic inventions, the phonograph and the incandescent electric light.

TELEPHONE AND PHONOGRAPH

By the time he moved to Menlo Park, Edison's name was well-known among both technical experts and businessmen concerned with telegraph technology and related fields. At the new lab he continued working on improving the telegraph, and he also produced important

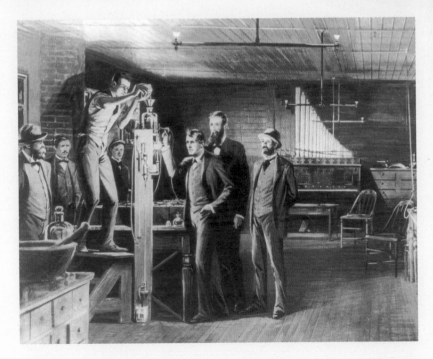

A moment in the development of the incandescent lamp in 1879. Edison, hand in pocket, watches intently.

inventions involving sound. For example, he made remarkable improvements in the telephone, which had been invented by the American Alexander Graham Bell in 1876. Edison developed a transmitter that was much better than Bell's and increased enormously the distances over which the telephone could be used to carry sound.

In mid-1877, Edison began thinking about a new sound-related device: the phonograph. He had already developed a device for recording Morse code telegraph signals. The telephone was a sort of telegraph that carried speech instead of Morse code, and Edison imagined that a recorder for it would be useful as well. He envisioned his new recording device as using a tiny point attached to a **diaphragm** (a material that vibrates in response to sound) to leave traces on a moving recording material. As sound caused the diaphragm to vibrate, the point would mark the sound patterns on the recording material. A sound recording could be played back by using it to make the point vibrate, thereby causing movements in the diaphragm, which would produce sound. The first working model of the phonograph was built before the end of 1877. For the recording material, Edison used tinfoil, which was wrapped around a tube, or cylinder, that was turned by hand.

The following year demonstrations of Edison's phonograph took place in the United States and Europe. In April, Edison traveled to Washington, D.C., where he showed the device to the National Academy of Sciences, members

One of the telephones developed by Edison

Edison with his phonograph during an 1878 trip to Washington, D.C., to demonstrate the device

of Congress, and President Rutherford Hayes. The phonograph provoked great interest among the public, and Edison himself regarded it as one of his favorite inventions—he called it his "baby" and thought it would "grow up to be a big feller and support me in my old age." But because Edison was busy with other matters, it was not until the late 1880s that he developed a commercially acceptable phonograph that could be sold to the public. When his "baby" did reach the market, his phonograph and record manufacturing operations did generate income for many years, as he had hoped. Sales were hurt, however, by Edison's reluctance to switch from the cylinder record to the increasingly popular disk format. Not until 1912 did his company introduce a disk phonograph and disk records.

Diagram of an early Edison incandescent lamp

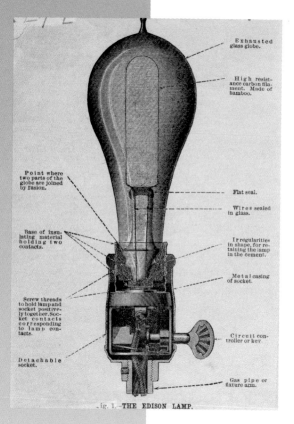

Exhausted glass globe.

High resistance carbon filament. Made of bamboo.

Point where two parts of the globe are joined by fusion.

Flat seal.

Wires sealed in glass.

Base of insulating material holding two contacts.

Irregularities in shape, for retaining the lamp in the cement.

Metal casing of socket.

Screw threads to hold lamp and socket positively together. Socket contacts corresponding to lamp contacts.

Detachable socket.

Circuit controller or key.

Gas pipe or fixture arm.

Fig. 1.—THE EDISON LAMP.

Electric lighting became a major focus of Edison's work in the late 1870s. So-called electric arc lights were already in use. In an **arc lamp** a current of electricity jumped across a gap between two wires to produce a glaringly bright light. Such light was suitable for purposes such as street lighting but not good for home use. Edison joined the hunt to develop an incandescent lamp, or a lamp in which a thin wire is heated until it gives off light. Developing a lamp in which the glowing wire would not melt or burn out quickly was an extremely difficult problem. Solving it depended not only on finding a suitable material for the wire, but also on discovering the best shape for the wire, the best type of bulb, and the best type of electricity, which could vary in characteristics such as voltage and amperage, to power the bulb.

The Menlo Park team experimented with all sorts of materials. The search was difficult and potentially dangerous. While working with nickel wires in late January 1879, Edison suddenly was forced to stop. He wrote in his notebook, "Owing to the enormous power of the light my eyes commenced to pain after seven hours' work, and I had to quit." He finally, in October 1879, succeeded in having a bulb work for about fourteen hours before burning out. It used a **filament**, or extremely thin wire, made of carbon. The bulb was not good enough to be sold to the public, but Edison and his assistants were enormously encouraged by what they had achieved.

Failure Is Sometimes Good

Edison often carried out an enormous number of experiments when he was studying a problem. Negative results didn't bother him, since he learned useful information from them—they taught him what wouldn't work, so he could look at other possibilities. As he put it, "I never quit until I get what I'm after. Negative results are just what I'm after. They are just as valuable to me as positive results." According to historian Paul Israel, who is an expert on Edison's life and work, Edison may have picked up his lack of fear of failure from his father. Samuel Edison was a jack-of-all-trades, and he usually was able to make enough money for his family to live on. But when a job or business venture didn't work out, the elder Edison readily moved on to some other effort. Israel said, "This sent a very positive message to his son—that it's okay to fail—and may explain why he rarely got discouraged if an experiment didn't work out."

Dynamo room of Edison's Pearl Street power station in New York City

Although Edison quickly filed for a patent on the carbon filament, the search for a better filament continued. Filaments made from carbonized Japanese bamboo proved particularly effective.

In addition to creating an effective incandescent lightbulb, Edison's team also worked out the details of producing and delivering electricity to thousands of homes and offices. A famous dynamo, or generator, that they devised in 1879—dubbed the "Long-Legged Mary Ann" (later known as "Long-Waisted Mary Ann")—used a pair of magnets each measuring nearly 5 feet (1.5 meters) in length and weighing over 500 pounds (225 kilograms).

The world's first commercial incandescent-lighting generating station was built by the Edison Electric Light Company at Holburn Viaduct in London, England. It went into operation in January 1882, providing power for about two thousand lamps. Meanwhile, Edison constructed a distribution system for an area of about one square mile (2.5 square kilometers) in New York City. The generating station for this system, located on Pearl Street, opened in September. Late that year,

DC and AC

Edison's system for generating and distributing electric power was carefully thought out, and it worked well. It used so-called **direct current** (DC), in which the **electric current** always flows in the same direction. Today, however, the power supplied to homes and businesses is usually not DC. Instead, most of them use **alternating current** (AC), in which the current changes direction many times each second. AC has certain advantages over DC. For example, it is much easier to transmit AC power over long distances.

Edison, who had begun to focus more on manufacturing and installation of the system than on research, closed his Menlo Park laboratory and opened a new lab in New York City.

MARY, MINA

William Leslie, the Edisons' third child, was born in October 1878. About six years later, in August 1884, Edison's wife Mary, who suffered from poor health for years, died. Edison's obsession with his work had kept him from spending much time with his family, but he was deeply affected by his wife's sudden death at the age of twenty-eight. His daughter Marion later spoke of how her father was "shaking with grief, weeping and sobbing so he could hardly tell me that Mother had died in the night."

In 1885, Edison met Mina Miller, a young, well-educated woman from Akron, Ohio. He already knew her father, Lewis Miller, who was a millionaire manu-

Glenmont, the Edison home in West Orange, N.J.

Edison experimented with electric locomotives. Here he drives his 1882 model.

Edison experimented with electric locomotives. Here he drives his 1882 model.

facturer and inventor of agricultural equipment. Edison and Mina were quite taken with each other, and they got married in February 1886 in Akron. Edison was thirty-nine, and his new wife twenty. The couple made their home on an estate called Glenmont that he had bought the month before the wedding. It was located in the Llewellyn Park area of West Orange. Following his wedding, Edison's focus on research once again sharpened,

Marriage by Morse Code

When Edison and Mina Miller were getting to know one another, he taught her Morse code so they could "talk" privately—by tapping in code in each other's hands—even when others were around. It was in this way that he proposed marriage to her while riding in a carriage with some other people. He later described the event: "I asked her thus in Morse code if she would marry me. The word 'yes' is an easy one to send by telegraphic signals, and she sent it. If she had been obliged to speak she might have found it much harder. Nobody knew anything about our long conversations. . . . If we had spoken words others would have heard them. We could use pet names without the least embarrassment, although there were three other people in the carriage."

Even the hard-working Edison sometimes took time off. Shown here: a fishing trip with one of his sons.

and in early 1887, he bought land in West Orange for a major new laboratory. As in his first marriage, Edison tended to spend more time at work than at home. But he apparently loved "Billie," as he called Mina. He wrote in one her books, "Mina Miller Edison is the sweetest little woman who ever bestowed love on a miserable homely good for nothing male."

The Edison Effect

Edison is famous for his achievements as an inventor, but he made at least one important scientific discovery: the Edison effect, also called thermionic emission. This effect consists in the fact that incandescent materials give off, or emit, electrons, which are the fundamental carriers of electric charge in electric current. The effect is the basis for electron tubes, including television picture tubes. Edison first noticed the effect in 1880 during his work on incandescent filaments and the electric light. Four years later he received a patent on an indicating device (for changes in output from electrical generators) that took advantage of the Edison effect. Because of thermionic emission's importance in electron tubes, and because Edison was the first to make use of the effect in an actual device, he is sometimes said to be the father of modern electronics.

CHAPTER 5

MOVIES AND MINING

Edison, at about age 65, with son Theodore, daughter Madeleine, and wife Mina

Edison planned for the West Orange lab to have "facilities incomparably superior to any other." He wrote in one of his notebooks, "Inventions that formerly took months & cost large sums can now be done 2 or 3 days with very small expense, as I shall carry a stock of almost every conceivable material." The lab, which opened in late 1887, was ten times bigger than the Menlo Park invention factory and was the birthplace of more than half of Edison's patents.

Births also took place in the Edison family. Mina and Tom Edison had three children: Madeleine, in May 1888; Charles, in August 1890; and Theodore Miller, in July 1898. Meanwhile, in 1896, Edison's father, Samuel, died at the age of ninety-two in Norwalk, Ohio.

MOTION PICTURES

In 1887, Edison started working on improvements for the phonograph, a project on which he remained active almost up to his death. As they did for the electric light, his labs and businesses developed and manufactured nearly everything needed, which in this case included records, record-making equipment, recording equipment, and playback devices. A phonograph factory was built near the laboratory.

Talking Doll

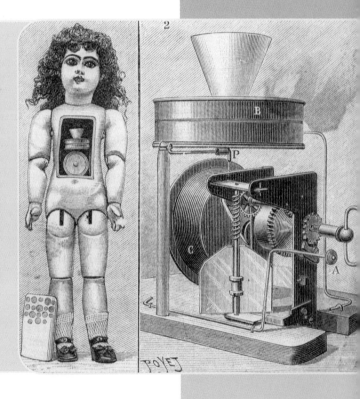

Among Edison's products connected with the phonograph was the talking doll. Each doll was about 2 feet (60 centimeters) tall; had a hat, a silk dress, and black shoes; and contained a little cylinder phonograph record of a song such as "Mary Had a Little Lamb," "Jack and Jill," or "Little Bo-Peep." The record turned out to be too delicate to survive the wear and tear of shipping, so in 1890, after several thousand dolls were made, production was stopped.

As often happened with Edison, working on one project gave him ideas for more inventions. His work on the phonograph got him thinking about a new project in a different area. In October 1888, he wrote, "I am experimenting upon an instrument which does for the Eye what the phonograph does for the Ear." Together with his employee W. K. L. Dickson, Edison developed a camera for making moving pictures and a **kinetoscope** for viewing them. The kinetoscope produced a tiny image, which was viewed through a peephole. Edison gave a demonstration of an early model in 1891.

Two years later a studio for making motion pictures was built at the West Orange lab. It was about 50 feet (15 meters) long, and its inside walls were black (so that the pictures would be sharper). The building was called the Black Maria (a common nickname for a police wagon, which the building was thought to resemble). The roof could be swung open to let sunlight in, and the entire building could be turned to follow the movement of the sun. Before it was torn down in 1903, the Black Maria was used to make hundreds of short movies, varying in length from a few seconds to up to a couple of minutes. The films showed everything from boxers, to dancers, to—in what was the first Western—cowboys and Indians. While Edison's work can be said to mark the beginning of the motion picture industry, many other people also started contributing to the industry's development, and Edison eventually withdrew from it.

METAL ORE

As early as the 1870s Edison thought about possible ways of processing cheap, low-quality metal ore to "concentrate" it into ore of useable quality. If the processing could be done inexpensively enough, then the resulting processed ore would cost less than high-quality ore that might have to be shipped from far

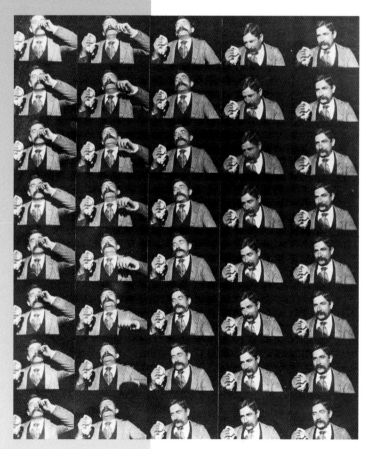

Edison's employee Fred Ott sneezing. This 1894 film was the first movie ever copyrighted.

Luck, Genius, and Perspiration

Edison once explained his research method to a newly hired employee at West Orange: "I do not believe in luck at all. And if there is such a thing as luck, then I must be the most unlucky fellow in the world. I've never once made a lucky strike in all my life. When I get after something that I need, I start finding everything in the world that I don't need—one damn thing after another. I find ninety-nine things that I don't need, and then comes number one hundred, and that—at the very last—turns out to be just what I had been looking for. It's got to be so that if I find something in a hurry, I git to doubting whether it's the real thing; so I go over it carefully and it generally turns out to be wrong. Wouldn't you call that hard luck? But I'm tellin' you, I don't believe in luck—good or bad. Most fellows try things and then quit. I never quit until I git what I'm after. That's the only difference between me, that's supposed to be lucky, and the fellows that think they are unlucky."

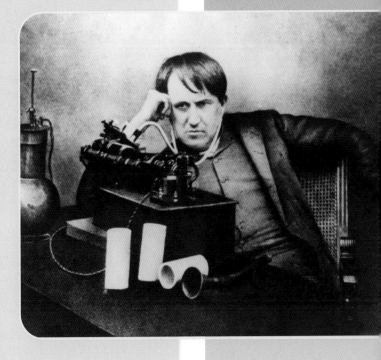

A famous 1888 photo shows Edison still at work after going seventy-two hours without sleep while trying to improve the phonograph.

"Then again," he went on, "a lot of people think that I have done things because of some 'genius' that I've got. That too is not true. Any other bright-minded fellow can accomplish just as much if he will stick like hell and remember that nothing that's good works by itself, just to please you; you've got to make the damn thing work. You may have heard people repeat what I have said, 'Genius is one per cent inspiration, ninety-nine per cent perspiration.' Yes, sir, it's mostly hard work."

away. As early as 1880, he applied for a patent on a method that used magnetism to concentrate low-grade ore. He launched a number of ore separation projects over the years. One of them occupied huge amounts of his time in the 1890s but turned out be his most spectacular failure. In an iron-mining area around Ogdensburg, in northern New Jersey, Edison built huge machines for concentrating low-grade iron ore. The project was tremendously expensive, and he sunk millions of dollars of his own money into it. This money came from the sale of much of his stock holdings and from the profits from his phonograph and motion picture businesses.

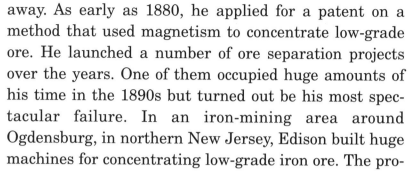

This modern crusher gives an idea of the massive size of the machinery used to process iron ore.

Despite years of effort, Edison was unable to bring the cost of concentrating the low-grade ore down far enough to compete with the naturally rich ore that was produced in the Lake Superior area. By the beginning of the twentieth century, he gave up on the project. Meanwhile, the stocks he sold to pay for the project had become very valuable. Unfortunately, he no longer owned them. Edison said, "Well, it's all gone, but we had a hell of a good time spending it." Edison simply enjoyed doing work he loved. Speaking of the iron ore project, he said, "I never felt better in my life than during the five years I worked here. Hard work, nothing to divert my thoughts, clear air, simple food made life very pleasant."

CEMENT AND BATTERIES

Although Edison's ore-concentrating project in northern New Jersey was a financial disaster, it was not a total loss. Edison had plenty of ideas for new projects. One of them—an innovative way for making **cement**—made productive use of some of the old equipment from the failed ore-concentrating venture. Another major new effort—an improved storage battery—earned Edison the most money of all his projects.

CEMENT HOUSE

The material called cement is the key component of concrete. (In many cases, concrete is often referred to simply as "cement.") Cement was coming into increasing use in the United States. In 1899, Edison designed a new kind of kiln, or oven, in order to more efficiently carry out the roasting process that is a key part of cement production. His kiln, which was much longer than existing ones, was a success. By the 1920s, the Edison Portland Cement Company was one of the top cement manufacturers in the United States. (Portland cement is a name for a particular type of cement.)

Edison, in 1910, with a model of the cement house

Edison dreamed up new uses for cement in order to help increase sales. Some of his ideas, such as the concrete piano, never made it into production. Others, such as a cement phonograph cabinet, did. He developed a cement house that could be constructed quickly and at very low cost. Liquid cement was poured into iron molds. After the building material had hardened, the molds were removed, and the house was almost complete; only things such as windows, doors, and furniture still needed to be added. Several cement houses were built, but the idea did not quickly catch on. Edison's cement house was probably too far ahead of its time.

A BETTER BATTERY

At the end of the nineteenth century, automobiles, whether powered by electricity or by fuels such as gasoline, were still very primitive. Edison thought cars powered by electricity, which was supplied to them by rechargeable storage batteries, had a promising future. But the storage batteries of the time were not very good: they were heavy, they were difficult to recharge, and they contained acid, which tended to eat away metal parts. Edison resolved to make a better battery that would use a less-corrosive "alkaline" substance of some sort instead of acid. Finding the right materials for the job turned out to be a difficult task. It took Edison roughly a decade—and thousands of experiments—to achieve a practical alkaline storage battery.

When *Harper's* magazine reported on Edison's project in its May 1901 issue, it said that "the famous inventor" considered his new storage battery "the most famous of all his creations" and believed that it would "revolutionize the whole system of transportation." But the gasoline-powered automobile underwent rapid

Young Inventor Encouraged by Hero

In 1896, Henry Ford, the future founder of the Ford Motor Company, was a young engineer with the Detroit Edison Company and an aspiring car inventor. In June of that year, he completed his first simple gasoline-powered vehicle. A couple of months later at a meeting of the Association of Edison Illuminating Companies, Henry Ford met Edison, whom he had long idolized. Although Edison did not always treat novice inventors kindly, he listened to the young man and asked him questions about his project. Edison was apparently pleased with what Ford said. The older inventor slammed the table with his fist and said, "Young man, that's the thing! You have it! . . . Keep at it."

Henry Ford in an early automobile

improvement, and by the time Edison finally perfected his alkaline storage battery, people's interest in cars powered by electricity was declining. Edison's battery failed to bring about the radical change in transporta-

Edison and a Baker electric car. The inventor holds one of his batteries that are used to power the vehicle.

tion for which he hoped, but it did find many uses—in, to give a few examples, submarines, backup power supplies, ship lighting and radios, and railroad lighting, signals, and switches—and, thus, turned out to be an extremely profitable product.

Quality Control

While working on his battery project, Edison was concerned to make his product as safe and durable as possible. This required considerable testing. One day in 1904, the inventor Tom Robins, who was visiting Edison at the West Orange lab, was startled by a series of loud crashes. Robins told the story that, after the crashes, a worker came and reported to Edison, "Second floor O.K., Mr. Edison." Edison then said, "Try the third floor." It turned out that Edison was having packages of storage batteries thrown out a window to see if they could withstand hitting the ground. Robins said, "For a scientist, Edison used some mighty peculiar methods."

FAME

In 1904, the United States celebrated the twenty-fifth anniversary of the invention of the carbon-filament incandescent lightbulb and central-power-station system by the man whom the *New York World* called "Our Greatest Living American, The Foremost Creative and Constructive Mind of This Country, Our True National Genius." A World's Fair held that year in St. Louis, Missouri, featured exhibits devoted to Edison's achievements. The American Institute of Electrical Engineers honored him with a banquet on his birthday, an event that continued to receive national attention in later years. Edison's achievements were not the sort usually recognized by Nobel Prizes, but in 1909, Sweden's Royal Academy of Sciences (which awards the Nobel Prizes in physics and chemistry) gave him a gold medal honoring his inventions in connection with the incandescent light and the phonograph.

The St. Louis World's Fair of 1904 showcased the technological marvels of the time, including electric lighting.

CHAPTER 7

"THE GREATEST LIVING AMERICAN"

In a 1913 survey of readers of the magazine *Independent*, Edison topped a list of "the most useful Americans." In a 1922 poll by the *New York Times*, he was named "The Greatest Living American." People wanted to hear Edison's opinion on almost any subject under the Sun, and he was often happy to oblige. Even his vacations were news, particularly a series of camping trips he took more or less every year for a period beginning in 1916. Part of what interested people was that Edison camped in the company of other well-known figures of the day, such as tire manufacturer Harvey Firestone, automobile maker Henry Ford, and nature writer John Burroughs. One of the participants on his

Edison's fame helped sell products, as in this 1916 ad.

1921 trip was U.S. president Warren G. Harding. Edison's friends Firestone and Ford encouraged him to undertake his last major research effort: a search for a new source of rubber for tires and other products.

Government Service

When World War I began in 1914, the United States at first stayed out of the fighting, not entering the war until 1917. Edison, however, publicly urged that the nation be prepared for fighting, should it become necessary, and he called for the creation of a military research laboratory. In 1915, the secretary of the Navy named him to head an advisory body called the Naval Consulting Board, which would review inventions that could be of use for national defense. After the United States entered the war, Edison devoted himself nearly full-time to naval research, working on problems such as how to detect submarines. He proposed a few dozen projects, but none of them were adopted. A military laboratory, the Naval Research Laboratory, was finally set up in 1920. Edison's suggestion that it be placed under civilian control, however, was rejected, and he resigned from the National Consulting Board early the next year.

QUEST FOR RUBBER

In the 1920s, rubber was an increasingly important material in manufacturing. Tires were made from it, and Edison used it for insulation in his storage batteries. The problem for the United States was that rubber supplies were primarily under the control of foreign countries. The substance was derived from certain plants, and a practical form of artificial, or synthetic, rubber had not yet been invented. In 1927, Edison—although

The aging Edison suffered health problems but worked as much as he could.

he was already eighty years old and in poor health—began searching for a way of making rubber from plants found in the United States. Botany, or the study of plants, was not a field in which he had any significant experience, but he attacked the problem with his usual thoroughness. Edison devoted several acres of land at his winter home in Fort Myers, Florida, to growing plants. He then launched a far-reaching search for promising plants, testing thousands of different types. Edison identified goldenrod as particularly suitable for making rubber, but his research was cut short by his death in 1931. The need for another source of rubber was later met by the development of synthetic rubber.

FINAL RESPECTS

Over the course of Edison's life, he collected awards from numerous countries, including Chile, France, Great Britain, Italy, Japan, and Russia. In 1928, he received the U.S. Congressional Medal of Honor.

The old Menlo Park invention factory was carefully reconstructed at a museum park called Greenfield Village that automaker Henry Ford created in Dearborn, Michigan. The fiftieth anniversary of

Congressional Medal

In 1928, Edison received the Congressional Medal of Honor in a ceremony at West Orange. U.S. president Calvin Coolidge took part from the White House via a national radio hookup. Coolidge said, "Although Edison belongs to the world, the United States takes pride in the thought that his rise from humble beginnings and his unceasing struggle to overcome the obstacles on the road to success illustrate the spirit of our country."

Secretary of the Treasury Andrew W. Mellon commented, "So fast and varied have been his contributions to its use that there are some men who even believe that electricity itself is merely another one of Edison's inventions."

Edison's invention of the incandescent electric light was celebrated in 1929 with a nationally broadcast ceremony at Greenfield Village. The event featured a dinner in Edison's honor that was attended by U.S. president Herbert Hoover, billionaire John D. Rockefeller Jr., Nobel Prize-winning scientist Marie Curie, and airplane inventor Orville Wright.

Edison died on October 18, 1931. At the request of President Hoover, Americans darkened their lights for a minute at 10 P.M. Eastern Time on October 21, the day of the great inventor's funeral. Radio networks observed a minute of silence.

To honor Edison, a huge tower was built at the site of his Menlo Park invention factory. The structure is topped with this 14-foot (4.3-meter) lightbulb.

TIMELINE

1847	Thomas Alva Edison is born on February 11 in Milan, Ohio
1854	Family moves to Port Huron, Michigan
1863	Begins a series of jobs as a telegraph operator that over a four-year period take him to cities in Canada and the Midwestern, Southern, and Eastern United States
1869	Receives first patent, for an automatic electric vote-counting machine
1870	Establishes a factory and laboratory in Newark, N.J.
1871	Marries Mary Stilwell
1873	First daughter, Marion Estelle ("Dot"), is born in Newark
1876	Edison builds laboratory at Menlo Park, N.J.; first son, Thomas Alva Jr. ("Dash"), is born
1877	Develops an improved transmitter for the telephone (invented the preceding year by Alexander Graham Bell) and invents the phonograph
1878	Edison's second son, William Leslie, is born
1879	Develops the first successful electric incandescent light
1882	Opens Pearl Street power station in New York City
1884	Wife, Mary, dies
1886	Marries Mina Miller
1887	Builds laboratory at West Orange, N.J.
1888	Second daughter, Madeleine, is born
1890	Builds iron ore concentration plant near Ogdensburg, N.J.; third son, Charles, is born
1891	Demonstrates the kinetoscope, a device for viewing motion pictures, designed with his employee, William Dickson
1898	Fourth son, Theodore Miller, is born
1899	Begins experimentation on storage batteries
1927	Launches effort to develop a process for producing rubber from plants native to the United States.
1931	Dies on October 18 in West Orange at the age of eighty-four.

alternating current (AC): electric current that reverses direction many times a second

arc lamp: a lamp that produces an extremely bright light as a result of the flow of electricity between the ends of two wires that are separated by a gap

cement: a fine, powdery material that is the key component of concrete; the word "cement" is sometimes also used to refer to concrete itself

diaphragm: a thin, flexible material that vibrates in response to electric signals to produce sound or vibrates in response to sound to produce electric signals

direct current (DC): electric current that always flows in the same direction

dynamo: a machine that generates direct-current from mechanical energy

electric current: a flow of electric energy, carried by tiny particles called electrons

filament: a very thin wire or strip in an incandescent lightbulb; when heated by electricity passing through it, the filament gives off light

incandescent lamp: an electric lightbulb that produces light when the filament inside it is heated by the passage of electricity; "incandescence" is the production of light as a result of being heated to a high temperature

kinetoscope: an early device for showing moving pictures, which are viewed through a peephole

Morse code: a code for sending telegraph messages that uses combinations of dots and dashes to represent letters and numbers

ore: rock from which metal is extracted

patent: the exclusive legal right to make or sell an invention

storage battery: a rechargeable device containing chemicals whose action produces electricity

technology: the study and use of devices, machines, and techniques for useful purposes

telegraph: a device for communication using electric signals that are transmitted over wires

TO FIND OUT MORE

BOOKS

Collins, Theresa M., and Lisa Gitelman. **Thomas Edison and Modern America: A Brief History with Documents (Bedford Series in History and Culture)**. Boston: Bedford/St. Martin's, 2002.

Delano, Marfe Ferguson. **Inventing the Future: A Photobiography of Thomas Alva Edison**. Washington, D.C.: National Geographic Society, 2002.

Davis, L. J. **Fleet Fire: Thomas Edison and the Pioneers of the Electric Revolution**. New York: Arcade, 2003.

Parker, Steve. **Thomas Edison and Electricity (The Science Discoveries Series)**. New York: Chelsea House, 1995.

Sullivan, George. **Thomas Edison (In Their Own Words)**. New York: Scholastic, 2002.

Tagliaferro, Linda. **Thomas Edison: Inventor of the Age of Electricity (Lerner Biography)**. Minneapolis: Lerner, 2003.

INTERNET SITES

Edison Birthplace Museum
http://www.tomedison.org
Describes the place where Edison was born and lived as a young boy and summarizes his family background.

Edison National Historic Site
http://www.nps.gov/edis/home.htm
Official Web site sponsored by the U.S. National Park Service. Among other things, it offers background information, photographs, virtual tours of Edison's West Orange laboratory and his Glenmont estate, and examples of early recordings and early Kinetoscope films.

Henry Ford Museum & Greenfield Village
http://www.hfmgv.org/exhibits/edison/
Information and pictures relating to Edison and his work. The Henry Ford Museum & Greenfield Village, in Dearborn, Michigan, is a vast park-museum that includes a reconstruction of Edison's laboratory at Menlo Park, N.J.

Library of Congress: Inventing Entertainment
http://memory.loc.gov/ammem/edhtml/edhome.html
An online collection of many early sound recordings and movies produced by the Edison companies.

INDEX *(continued)*

About the Author

Richard Hantula has written and edited books and articles on science, medicine, and health for more than two decades. He was the senior U.S. editor for the Macmillan Encyclopedia of Science. Born in Michigan, he has lived in New York City since the late 1970s.

DATE DUE

HIGHSMITH 45230